LEADERSHIP

How to Lead Effectively, Efficiently, and Vocally in a Way People Will Follow!

Second Edition: *Expanded and Updated!*

DEREK STANZMA

"Leadership: How to Lead Effectively, Efficiently, and Vocally in a Way People Will Follow"

Selected, Compiled & Edited by Derek Stanzma 2014

Copyright © June 2014 by Derek Stanzma

Why I Wrote This Book

There are numerous reasons for why I wrote this book. None more pressing however, than the simple fact that the world needs leaders. Not just any leaders mind you. Strong leaders. Articulate leaders. Effective leaders. Leaders who are tough, forceful, yet encouraging.

I personally have had many people around me assume the role of leadership. Some effectively... others not. Over time I began to learn and take note of what I naturally looked for in leaders. I also learned what I didn't like. Unfortunately, I found myself disliking those in leadership roles more often than I found I liked them. I found myself scared, abandoned, shamed, forgotten, angry, unimpressed, unamused, and most importantly... unmotivated!

I began to think to myself *"why is it that people can't seem to grasp the concept of how to lead properly?"*, and then it hit me... I am a natural born leader.

Now I don't say that to brag or boast in any way, shape, or form. Instead I say it because, whether I like it or not, and trust me sometimes I most definitely do NOT, I am a born leader.

What that means is leading people comes more naturally to me than most. I don't have to think about what to say, or how to say things, in order to get people motivated and be more productive. It is a gift of mine, rather than a skill. But luckily the skill of leadership is just as effective as the gift of leadership, and more importantly, skills can be learned.

That is my main purpose behind this book. It is to use what I have learned through my years under and in leadership roles in order to teach others the most effective, efficient, and productive ways to motivate and lead people in the way that makes them **want** to follow.

I can't make any guarantee's, but it is my most sincere hope that by the end of this book you will find yourself properly equipped with the skills and knowledge necessary to make your team, workplace, or following productive, efficient, and most of all... MOTIVATED!

Table of Contents

Introduction

I want to thank you and congratulate you for downloading the book, "Leadership: How to lead Effectively, Efficiently, and Vocally in a Way People Will Follow!"

We encounter various leaders in different walks of life. We work with our managers at work, who lead from the front and become the leaders that guide us in our work life.

Life can have a lot of pleasant surprises and one of them could be you becoming one such leader. Of course, if the responsibility to lead has been bestowed upon you, you have inherent qualities that sum up a leader. However, learning is a continuous process and the same applies when you are a leader.

You can never be an effective leader unless you keep an open mind to learn and excel along the way. Through this eBook, we have compiled a list of different attributes of being a leader, which will help you in forming and up-skilling yourself into an effective leader.

This eBook contains proven steps and strategies on how to lead effectively and efficiently. It illustrates how one can lead with a vision, and end up leaving a legacy.

In the following chapters you'll learn whether leaders are born or made, what people look in their leaders, what are the marks of a leader, how leaders make decisions, how they bring out the best in people, how they strategize, how they lead with your heart and also show you how to become the leader you always wanted to be.

But most importantly, you will learn how to manage change in your life with poise, and discernment. So sit back and relax and finally learn how to lead the way you want to.

Chapter 1: Are Leaders Born or Made?

"If your actions inspire others to dream more, learn more, do more and become more, you are a leader."

- John Quincy Adams

This question has been asked countless number of times. And over the past decades, many people have debated over this subject. Are some people really born to become leaders while others, even with great effort, are doomed to remain followers? Or is leadership a skill that can actually be learned and employed by people who want to make a difference? This question is still left without a definite answer. Are we pre-destined to become sheep and follow the herd, or contrastingly a shepherd, who leads the multitude? The debate is still ongoing.

Many people find it easier to think that some individuals were born with an innate capability to lead because they know about the great leaders who made a big difference in the world. Leaders such as Mahatma Gandhi, Abraham Lincoln, John F. Kennedy, Winston Churchill, Martin Luther King, Jr., and Nelson Mandela are a few of them. These men and a few others are known to have influenced huge masses to move forward into the modern world that we know of now.

These men had a certain charisma that drew people in, and made them stop and listen to what they had to say. They were able to penetrate straight to other people's hearts and lead them towards the innovation or the new ideologies that they wanted to pursue. Even with the passing of time, their contributions to humanity have not been forgotten but instead they are still celebrated and cemented in history.

"Leaders are made, they are not born. They are made by hard effort, which is the price which all of us must pay to achieve any goal that is worthwhile."
- Vince Lombardi

Many people still believe that good and effective leaders are made. Many of these effective leaders started out as regular "Joes" who wanted to make something good out of their lives. They dared to pursue the visions that have been implanted into their minds with the passion bellowing in their hearts. They may not have all the necessary leadership skills at the onset but they pursued and learned from their mistakes and their experiences. They were committed to bringing the people they lead towards their goals. When they fail, they are the first one to stand up and try again. They inspire their subordinates to do the same until their goal has been achieved.

Humanity would not have reached the progress we enjoy now if man had only relied on the innate leadership of a very few number of people. Very few people start out with the modesty, compassion, and determination required to become a good leader. Many of the advancements we enjoy now are the fruits of the leadership of ordinary men who dreamed big for themselves and for their fellowmen. These seemingly ordinary men worked hard to develop their leadership qualities that helped them inspire the people they worked with. They braved all the hardships required to achieve success in whatever field they chose to excel in.

If you are reading this eBook and wondering if you were born a leader or not, you need to understand that you can become whatever you choose to become. Your efforts in learning how to become a better leader even shows that you have what it takes to become one. Many good leaders before you started out as simple, ordinary men. They all came from various circumstances – some were born into a rich family while others were born in poverty.

Some of them have multiple titles at the end of their names while others have barely attended any formal schooling. But they all had one thing in common – no matter what challenges they were facing, they found the courage to overcome those challenges to achieve success and make the world a better place at the same time. With that knowledge, I hope that you now believe that you can transform yourself into a good leader who can make a difference.

Chapter 2: Start with a Vision

"The very essence of leadership is that you have to have a vision. It's got to be a vision you articulate clearly and forcefully on every occasion. You can't blow an uncertain trumpet."

- Reverend Theodore Hesburgh

Leadership is all about getting from point A to point B. Leaders exist to direct a group of people to a better place. That better place can mean different things for different people. Leaders lead their people towards success, abundance, freedom or simple happiness. But the destination has to be absolutely clear to the leader himself in order for him to lead his subordinates to that new place.

`Would you tell me, please, which way I ought to go from here?'– said Alice in Wonderland.
`That depends a good deal on where you want to get to,' said the Cat.
`I don't much care where--' said Alice.
`Then it doesn't matter which way you go,' said the Cat.

The Cat in Alice in Wonderland clearly stated it. It doesn't matter which way a leader goes if he or she doesn't care or doesn't know where he wants to go. A good leader will only be able to discern the right path if he or she has a clear vision of the destination. That vision will enable the leader to build trust, teamwork, and motivation and shared responsibilities amongst his subordinates.

Along the way, you as a leader will have to face a lot of choices. You will have to make a lot of decisions not only for yourself but for your team as a whole. Having a clear vision will help you determine the right direction you and your team have to take. You would not need to wait for any sign or provocation from other people to move. You will be able to think for yourself and your team to find the ways, on how you can change your visions into reality.

Turn Your Vision into Reality

Having a vision doesn't just mean defining the ultimate goal you want to achieve. To become a better leader, your vision should encompass more than the dream itself. It should include an extensive knowledge of who you and your team are. What are your strengths? What are your weaknesses? Do you and your team lack any skills that will help you achieve your goals? Do you and your team need to work on eliminating some weaknesses that may hinder you from making your vision a reality? You need to know what values are important for you and your team.

After having a clear vision and knowing more about you and your team, the next step is to find the best ways on how to achieve your goals. Your vision will not become a reality at a snap of a finger. You need to find the correct path towards your goals. If no path is currently available, you should find the courage and confidence to create a new one. Your vision is nothing when it is not backed by a solid plan and properly communicated to the team. Your subordinates will enthusiastically follow you as their leader if they know where you plan to lead them.

You also need to remember that your vision is something that you need to keep alive. It is not enough that you lay it out to your team in the beginning. It is important to remind them about it every day so they will not lose focus on what is important for your team. The more you and your team are able to focus on your goals, the clearer the vision becomes and the deeper it stays in their hearts.

Live the dream. Once you have identified the vision you want to turn into reality, ask yourself to live it at once. Every day, you need to act as if whatever you have envisioned is already happening. Your daily actions should be in harmony with your vision. And when your subordinates and the other people you deal with see you living the dream, they will then believe how serious you are with your vision. Seeing your commitment to the dream, the people around you will also feel committed to achieving it.

Let your vision be the foundation of your team or organization. If ever you any encounter any problem or obstacle, go back to your vision and strengthen your commitment to achieve it. Know that the problem or obstacle right in front of your are just some of the things you need to get through in order to advance towards your goals. If you need to change your route, do so. But make sure that the change in route will still lead you to your goals. Accept problems and changes as part of the process. Be ready to face them knowing that you and your team have what it takes to make your vision a reality. Your commitment to your vision will make a big difference in your success.

Chapter 3: Bring out the Best in People

"Outstanding leaders go out of their way to boost the self-esteem of their personnel. If people believe in themselves, it's amazing what they can accomplish."

- Sam Walton

A leader leading from the front is a passé. It is no more a herd, but a group of individuals who have different skills, motivational levels and thinking. Modern day people management is dynamic and has working patterns which are ever changing and demanding. So the leader leads by example - by being part of the initiative, imparting the change and on the whole getting the best out of every individual.

Being a leader, you may have choices to lead a team which already exists - where your job is to motivate and get the best out of them. Or you may just have to select a team, chalk out a plan and implement it as well. In both the cases, you will come up with a strategy which fits your ultimate goal i.e. leading them and getting the job done. On the other hand, you may be required to look at external perspectives like the market dynamics and its effects on your business while assigning jobs and leading a team.

Adoption and Motivation

Firstly, you need to be part of the group, understand the group philosophy and adopt certain prevailing tactics of the group in order to get the best out of them. By doing so, you not only win their confidence, but will also become one among them. In the process, you will understand their strengths and limitations as a team and as individuals.

Secondly, as part of adoption, you will create your need by giving them crucial inputs at appropriate times and resolve any problems that may arise in due course. This may happen only when you understand and adopt certain tendencies of the group. And when the mutual chord strikes, people relate themselves to you and find value in you. This becomes the first step for you to lead them and get the best out of them.

Every individual has a different set of motivational factors. After being part of them, you need to understand what motivates them to give their best. They may have a group philosophy and emotions behind them or simply get motivated when you boost their self esteem.

As a leader, you need to strategize and work out plans which are both common and unique. For a few, it might be the future vision and value they share with you, so they get motivated by every move you make. And for the rest, it may be direct and indirect benefits, or just a sizable incentive which is given for completing a particular task.

One of the common motivation factors among a group of people or a team could be, group tactics preceding over individual thinking. Within the group, you will find people who have the tendency to follow others – if the group members are happy and get motivated about some initiatives the leader takes the others also will follow blindly since the group adheres to it.

So as a leader, you will identify that common factor and use it as a motivational tool to obtain the best out of them.

Visualising the inside out

Once you emerge as a leader, one of the strengths you ought to have is visualizing every individual's current and future capabilities. While working with them, you will know who is best at what and how they will shape up in the future. You could assign them roles based on their current capability and future growth by visualizing their future prospects. This could be a motivational factor to get the best out of every individual, as they see the trust you carry in them.

Every individual has limitations, as a leader you will compliment by identifying these limitations and convert them into possible strengths. When you know them in and out, the road map becomes very clear and predictive. And if something doesn't happen you will know the reasons behind it. Further, you will be able to understand why an individual is unable to perform or how an individual is performing better.

As a leader, it is essential for you to understand that every individual has a saturation point and they tend to lose momentum for causes unknown. Before anyone does, you should be the first person to identify the cause and find ways to constantly motivate the individual. If need be, you need make them shift gears as your final objective is to make them succeed.

Unlocking Potential

Your growth as a leader becomes stronger when you are able to identify and unlock every individual's potential. You will not only improve the team's performance but also elevate yourself as a leader when you unlock the strengths of every individual. The first question you need to ask yourself is 'are you prepared to unlock their potential?', because if you are not prepared or if you have not learned the trade secrets, then you will just be shooting in the dark.

Learning becomes an integral part of any stage, so you need to be prepared to understand every aspect of the individual when you try to unlock their potential. Firstly, if it is a common initiative you need to ensure that you pick up the right kind of person based on their skills, knowledge and understanding of the initiative. Secondly, if you are sure about what you need and what they have, you can set expectations accordingly based on listing key outcomes.

Thirdly, motivate the individual constantly by working on their strengths so that your outcome matches the best what they have. And finally, you have to have a development plan for every individual so that they have a clear understanding of why they are working and what they are working for.

Nurture and Enhance

Everyone needs peak performance and performers in their companies. Given the current market scenario, much time goes in identifying top talent, smart performers and in retaining them. Well at times it becomes impossible for you as a leader to keep pace with the changing dynamics both internal and external. In this kind of scenario an effective leader focuses on nurturing and enhancing talent of the individuals.

You may be the coach of a world class football team or a leader of a group, but the key to success is in nurturing and enhancing the individual's performance which finally elevates the organization or the team's performance. Irrespective of the pressures in the daily working scenario the simple way to nurture them is to 'keep the joy and thrill' of working even in the daily routine. The moment you are able to create this magic they will find even the routine jobs interesting. Keep them engaged most of the time, be it work or play.

A positive leader has a positive surrounding and a positive impact. It is imperative that as a leader you always have a positive vision. It is proven that a positive vision will have higher levels of motivation for the team and individuals to outperform in any situation. They tend to take up the everyday challenges and deal with them positively, because as a leader they see you very positive and they see you before the vision.

Finally, you should create a platform where every individual has a scope to learn on a continuous basis. It should ultimately become a culture and a habit that every individual is nurtured so that their performance is enhanced through continuous learning.

Well Informed

A thoughtful leader is always well informed about whatever is happening in the market. The best way is to identify and understand the latest trends and share the news with the team on a regular basis so that they have a learning input always from your end. At the same time, as a leader you should contribute to the external world by sharing your expertise so that you get recognition in the market about who you are which in turn elevates your image as leader in your team.

Giving Space

To motivate your team and get the best out of them, you have to give them the space, which they need both on the personal and professional front. All work and not play makes jack, you me and every one dull. So as a leader, you understand their priorities and respect them for what they are. By doing so, you will not only get the best out of them, but also make them stick to you and your ideologies.

It is good to motivate them and that depends on how you do it. Seldom, people think motivation as bothering factor or an interference in their job if it is on a regular basis. Many instances where we come across, the simple question of 'hey how is it going on' is perceived as a follow up, because you are the person who has given the job and you need to trust and give that space to the individual to perform well. You have to get involved only when they need you or if there is an issue to be addressed at your level.

A commonly accepted process

If you see success in implementing a process, it is advisable that you replicate the same thing with either a different individual or the other part of the group. That way it becomes more effective and acceptable and individuals will start feeling that they have something in common to follow. When you want the team to perform well and you want every individual to exceed expectations, in the initial stages you would not want to invent processes at every stage. Rather the best way is to go with what is a proven and accepted one and be done with it.

You think differently - then you are part of my team

Diverse thinking, different opinions and creating a platform to brainstorm are the best ways to motivate and improve teams and an individual's performance. If you cannot think differently, then you have lesser chances of becoming an effective leader. Likewise if you don't have people who can think differently and out of the box, you will have limited scope to create a winning team, which literally eliminates the possibility of getting the best out of them.

You need to constantly innovate if you wish to be part of this race to success. As a leader you need to imbibe this culture in the team and allow everyone to come up with ideas, be it best or not the best – you have allowed them to speak up.

Make them say 'We did it'

The best trait of a leader is when people say 'we did it'. While you played the sheet anchors role in making them achieve their goals, if they succeed the success is a shared vision which you and they had all the time. There may be an extraordinary achievement the team or an individual had, as a leader you need to identify and compliment it appropriately and make them feel they did it. It becomes a source of inspiration for them even if it is a small contribution which they made and you recognized it as their leader. When they feel they did it, they will go to any extent to impress you as their leader and will follow you on any initiative you will drive in the future.

The surprise Elements

How about an ice breaker in between a session or a task, a team outing or just a huge round of applause in between tight schedules and brainstorming meetings? You could use all your creative thoughts and mind you all of them may work. You will be surprised to know the craziest of the ideas work well at times, because on a stressful day, you would want a bit of relaxation than getting tips on how to work better.

Chapter 4: Lead with Your Heart

"I suppose leadership at one time meant muscles; but today it means getting along with people."

- Mahatma Gandhi

Many people were taught to practice leadership with their heads and not with their hearts. This is especially true for leaders in the corporate world. Many old fashioned Chief Executive Officers (CEOs) are accustomed to putting the welfare of the business before the well being of the employees who work for the company. Many business leaders take pleasure in being described as tough, strong-minded, ultra-rational and results driven. They don't care to be called compassionate, benevolent, generous and kind.

But times are changing. Many modern leaders and CEOs are now realizing how important compassion is in leading their teams and organizations into greater heights. These new leaders now believe that they should not only lead with their heads but also with their hearts. They believe that their subordinates will be more willing to follow them if they feel their leaders have compassion. The new leaders now understand that their subordinates are human beings too who have their own thoughts and feelings. They now strive to bring inspiration into the workplace instead of just laying down hard and fast rules with no room for compassion.

Leaders who employ a compassionate style of leadership can be described as follows:

1. Compassionate leaders are in tune with their own feelings and emotions. Their thoughts, words and actions are all aligned. They find time to talk and connect with the other people in the team. They understand that the feelings and emotions that they bring to the workplace do not only affect them but everyone around them.

1. Compassionate leaders take the effort to control over their moods. Whatever circumstances they find themselves and no matter how many problems they are facing, they are able to maintain a positive outlook in life. They let their own optimism inspire other people. They do not allow negative and demotivating feelings to creep in – both in them and amongst the team members.

2. People are more important to them than procedures. They always find better ways on how to do things to make sure that everyone in the team is working effectively. They sincerely care for the well-being of everyone they work with and they make sure that everyone's needs are taken care of, as much as possible. Compassionate leaders are receptive towards other people's thoughts and emotions.

3. Compassionate leaders always remain hopeful. They passionately and persistently inspire other people to move towards their shared vision. They motivate their subordinates to always remain positive, energized and filled with hope despite the problems and obstacle that come their way.

4. Compassionate leaders connect with other people through honest and open dialogues. They emphasize honesty, openness and truthfulness within the organization. They encourage not only their managers but the subordinates as well to speak candidly when they have something to say. They believe that truth and candidness when applied with modest, respect and conviction can make the team work better.

"People don't quit companies. They quit managers."
- Anonymous

Managers and other leaders in the workplace seldom fail because they lack technical expertise. More often, they do not become successful as leaders because they lack human relations skills that can enable them to connect with the people they work with. Research studies have shown that more and more employees quit their jobs because they did not like how they were treated by their superiors. Many of them relate that they are not satisfied with their jobs because of the quality of their relationship with their bosses. With this in mind, you should assess yourself to see if you have the required human relations skills that can make you a better leader.

Good leaders do not just work hard to reach a high level of emotional intelligence. They also make the effort to understand the behaviors of the other members in the team. They understand that each person in the team is unique in their own way and encourage the team to celebrate their differences. A good leader knows that these differences need not bring chaos into the team. Instead, he finds ways on how to take advantage of the team's diversity and advance it further towards their goals. A good leader continuously tries to learn how to manage conflicts inside and outside of his organization.

There is no doubt that a lot of leaders have great ideas that they willingly share with everyone in the team. But a good leader is differentiated from most leaders because of their ability to listen to what other people have to say. Good leaders encourage their subordinates to speak up and share their thoughts and opinions. They take into consideration the different points of view of the team when making plans. They know that even those in the lowest levels can have effective ideas that can help the team achieve their goals.

Here are some simple techniques you can use to improve your human relations skills:
1. Be generous with your compliments and praises. Always be appreciative of your team's efforts.
2. When you have to criticize or argue, do it considerately.

3. Give credit where credit is due. Your subordinates will become motivated if you share the limelight with them. Do not dwell too much on your own reputation. If your team succeeds, it will ultimately be reflected back at you.
4. Always try to be fair with everyone you work with. Remember that each member of your team is important in their own way.
5. Learn how to keep secrets.
6. Be humble. Admit it when you commit errors and mistakes. You will gain more respect when your subordinates see that you know how to acknowledge your own errors and mistakes.

Chapter 5: Marks of a Leader

"True leadership lies in guiding others to success. In ensuring that everyone is performing at their best, doing the work they pledged to do and doing it well."

- Bill Owens

With the changing times, the role of a leader too is fast changing. Just a couple of decades ago, leaders were mostly rational, unemotional and authoritarians. Of course, with the changing times, expectations from a leader have vastly changed. The good news is most leaders have adapted themselves to the changing work culture in organizations.

The mark of a leader in the 21st century is much different than the traditional role of a leader. But before getting to that, one has to understand there is a vast difference in the role of a leader and that of someone in power.

A person in power may have a fancy title and position for himself but he may not necessarily be a leader. A leader on the other hand is a person who has the influence over people and can change the course of a team due to the influence he has over the team. This influence combined with other qualities can attribute the 'Mark of a Leader'

Let us take a look at some of these aspects

Ethics and Integrity

When it comes to being a leader, you are responsible for an entire team of people. The first aspect of leadership is being able to lead ethically and honestly. Your entire team will look up to you to make the right decisions; hence you need to maintain the bar ethically high. This will ensure a healthy bonding within the team and also you will be able to influence everyone due to your excellent values and ethics. Integrity is the number one influencing factor; everyone likes to work with and for an ethical leader.

Effective Delegation

A leader's job is not doing things but getting the work done effectively from the team. Being a leader, the most important thing for you is to choose the right person for the right job and delegate the work accordingly. Effective delegation will ensure that the work output is efficient and has no or minimum errors. To effectively delegate, a leader should understand the strengths of each team member and accordingly capitalize on the strengths. Effective delegation will also improve the overall performance of the team and thereby improve the productivity of the business or organization.

Open Channel of Communication

A leader has to communicate with the team as well as the superiors on a daily basis. To get the right kind of output, a leader needs to effectively explain the task and communicate with the team and after the performance; he needs to explain the output to the management. He/she needs to be extremely strong with their communication. This doesn't stay limited to the leader; he/she should be able to influence the team members to effectively and openly communicate with each other. This will improve the trust factor within the team and reduce conflicts.

Inspire

It is extremely essential for a leader to be able to inspire his team members. Teams cannot perform tasks just by being told, they need to be inspired to see the bigger picture. A leader's vision needs to transform into an inspiration for the team when focusing towards the goal. There will be times when the team's morale will be low or when the performance is not up to the mark. The best way to change the scenario is to inspire the team members in newer ways. Acknowledging efforts and appreciating everyone for their hard work plays an extremely important role in motivating and inspiring employees.

Take Initiatives

Leaders are the first ones to volunteer and take initiatives. This quality sets them apart from the group and team. A leader shouldn't expect others to do or perform a certain task, which he/she is unwilling to do. He/she needs to lead from the front. They can create an impact in the mind of the team by doing taking initiatives and leading by example.

Maintaining the Morale

Inspiring and motivating the team is one of the basic expectations from a leader. However, there will be times when the morale of the team is pretty low and things may not go as per plan. This can negatively affect the output and the productivity of each employee. This is where the leader's role comes into play once again. He needs to ensure that the team's morale is high and the members are confident, he needs to maintain positivity within the team. For this, the leader himself should be confident and positive.

Chapter 6: Decision Making Skills

"A true leader has the confidence to stand alone, the courage to make tough decisions, and the compassion to listen to the needs of others. He does not set out to be a leader, but becomes one by the equality of his actions and the integrity of his intent"

- Douglas McArthur

Humankind can be divided into two sections, those who lead and those who follow. Those who lead are the leaders while those who follow are obviously the followers. But a leader cannot be simply called a person who leads or is in charge of or commands a certain group of people or followers. A leader is a person who can guide and direct his followers and people effectively on the way which will lead to the goals of that specific crowd or group. A leader effectively heads his/her people and leads them to success.

Various types of leaders exist according to sociology and social psychology. Though they are different on various minute levels, all of these leaders are ultimately people who can command and lead their people properly.

Technically, every human being on the surface of the earth should be able to lead. But it is well known that this sounds impossible and isn't seen in day to day life. Why? This is due to certain qualities and traits, known as the leadership qualities in corporate world, which make some people, stand out and let them be a leader.

These qualities include confidence in people, a charming personality and aura, a positive attitude, ability to adjust, intelligence, extroversion, decision making and various others skills that set them apart from others. All of these qualities essentially make a person a great leader. Out of these, decision making is one of the most important skills that is necessary for not only leaders but also other people who either aspire to be leaders or want to lead their lives successfully.

It is generally noticed that people who can make correct and appropriate decisions quickly and instantly are always on the top positions of their career ladder and are also quite popular in society. Thus it can be deduced that decision making is an extremely important personality trait. If a leader can lead his team with appropriate decisions to success, he/she'll enjoy leadership for a long time; else his/her reign would be drastically short.

In this fast growing world it is observed a lot of times that people lack decisive skills. These people also include a large number of leaders who cannot make successful decisions. This is a growing problem and due to this a large number of leaders fail to succeed. Decision making skills are quite easy to procure; anyone can develop good decisive skills. It is just a matter of experience and appropriate guidance.

The world envisions leaders who are successful and are clear and certain about things and ideas, it doesn't want leader who are hesitant or unsure of matters. It is not an easy task to do this, these types of decisions need understanding of change, uncertainty and unfortunate reactions from others. This is highly stressful. Thus the world envisions them to be one of those who can make challenging decisions and aren't shy to make strong and bold choices. Good leaders can make decisions, but best leaders can make correct decisions. They understand the subtle and dangerous balance between emotions and reason, and those who can keep these two equal are certainly the best leaders.

Decision making skills are based on three factors, which if developed can ultimately develop decisiveness as well. These three skills are
   1. Emotional Intelligence
   2. Managing Uncertainty
   3. Intuition
Let us have a look at all of these and understand them well

Emotional Intelligence

One of the biggest challenges which people as well as leaders face while making decisions is the power of emotions. Man is an emotion driven animal and nearly everyone gets influenced by their emotions. This sometimes leads to making inappropriate decisions just because the person was emotionally vulnerable at the moment. To make good strategic and long term decisions it is essential to know the skill of controlling ones emotions or at last making them subdued for time being.

Great leaders can accept their emotions and can ignore them properly so that they can make proper decision. This is the old mind over heart matter; a great leader listens to his heart but acts according to his mind. The leader should allow and accept the emotional reaction but should focus on facts and particulars.

Some people say that they stop feeling emotions for keeping their decisions accurate. This is quite impossible; not experiencing an emotion is like climbing a hill with your back towards the top. You may probably somehow reach the top, but the consequences you'll face while doing so will be brutal and time and energy consuming.

It will take herculean efforts and the results will be ultimately disappointing and not substantial enough. So instead of trying to suppress emotions the best thing is to experience it. You cannot kill emotions, but you can suppress its intensity and can make your factual prowess stronger. Emotional intensity tends to pass quickly and what is left is the clear substrates of facts which will make you think logically and will help you make best decisions. Remember, it is impossible to kill emotions or to get them out of the decision making process, so one must just keep them from taking over and be in control oneself.

Managing Uncertainty

It is a well known fact that making decisions is a hard and complex process. So why exactly making decisions is difficult? It can be deduced that people find making decisions complex because of the uncertainty involved. Human beings are afraid of outcomes; we are a species who are nervous about uncertainty. We don't like uncertainty; we as a species find it uncomfortable and disturbing. This is why we see people who spend hours and hours looking at every angle of a situation to try to reduce uncertainty as much as possible. This is highly energy as well time consuming. Not all situations permit people to take hours to choose something; most of the time a leader needs to make decision as soon as the situations arises.

People often face a situation like paralysis when they are confronted by uncertainty. They are highly confused and befuddled which affects their overall logic and calm. It is seen that a lot of people as well leaders make highly inaccurate decisions when they are confronted with uncertainty, even basing their decisions on things which aren't even related to the situation. This leads to decisions which can ruin careers. It is necessary for a leader to question the uncertainties.

Like mentioned earlier, we cannot repress our emotions. Uncertainty is also a form of emotion, and thus it cannot be repressed either. A great leader understands this and accepts uncertainty. He understands and accepts that it is not always necessary to resolve the uncertainties instead he should employ his time and energy on the best decisions. This is again an important quality which is actually a form of self control.

Though a leader avoids uncertainties, it doesn't mean that he doesn't analyze situations. Analyzing is also extremely important. Analysis can help a leader get and gain information which can prove to be highly beneficial in the overall decision making process. The key here is not spending too much time on analyzing and making it quick. Unless analyzing is quick the decision process will ultimately collapse. If a good leader gets stuck in these two things, he'll try to seek balance and probability and will choose the best decision as quickly as possible.

It is also essential to limit your choices. A good leader always tries have limited choices. Humans love to have various options because this creates a false sense of security that they can have a lot of things. But when forced to choose one, the human mind gets confused and thus goes into a chaotic state. By considering every alternative, we give ourselves a lot of choices and options which raises uncertainty. This uncertainty as shown above ultimately leads to the loss of time and energy. It is also possible that while looking to tackle uncertainty we somehow create more uncertainties, which again leads to more and thus a vicious cycle like thing is created which hinders decision making process.

There are a lot of studies which have proved that when people are confronted with multiple choices, say four or five, they take more time to decide and sometimes even opt to not choose any of the choice at all, thus avoid making decision. Ultimately it is essential to keep your choices limited, which will benefit the leader as well as his team mates.

Intuition

This may sound quite erratic and eccentric because intuition is supposed to be something which is not to be trusted. But a lot of great and successful leaders are ready to bet their hats on their gut feelings. Intuition is an essential sub conscious feeling which can definitely help you make correct and appropriate decisions.

The leaders who can work by their intuition are able to trust themselves thoroughly and are free to avoid the tedious cycle of over thinking which is obviously a great distraction and hindrance in the decision making process. The more a great leader understands and knows a subject, the more he can trust his intuition. He will find it more reliable and trust worthy. A leader should thus thrive to make himself an expert and master of his field so as to develop his intuition and save his time.

People who go by their gut feelings are proven to be happier with their decision as compared to those who analyzed and thought thoroughly over a decision. Rationalizing ourselves in anything is possible but the first impression is mostly our true feeling.

To hear and listen to your intuition is quite easy. It is the tiny voice in your head which appears when you are confronted with choices or are trying to judge things. It can be enhanced by doing meditative exercises and practices or things which calm you down, like reading, relaxing, walking your dog etc. These moments let you reflect yourself and this reflection is essential in intuition. Staying away from technology for a day to hone your thoughts and thinking is also very important.

These are the three skills of a leader who wants to hone his decision skills. Being a decisive person is a learning, which needs a lot of experience. One cannot simply be born with good decisive skills, they need to be developed and honed with time. Making changes in oneself is a vital quality of a great leader. Practice and constant vigilance can lead an average person on the way to become an exceptional leader. Stay calm, trust yourself and go make some decisions.

Chapter 7: Learn How to Manage Change

"Change will not come if we wait for some other person or some other time. We are the ones we've been waiting for. We are the change that we seek."

- Barack Obama

Change management is one basic skill that all good leaders should master. No business is spared from change. Everyone has to face it one time or another. A leader who does not know how to properly manage change is definitely doomed for failure.

When your company is faced with a change that you need to plan for and manage, you need to consider these five main principles of change management:

- **Different individuals respond to change in different ways.**

Some people prefer stability over change. If they have to choose, they want things to always stay the same way. They feel insecure when they feel that things are changing very quickly. But there are also people who can easily embrace change. These people are continuously craving for new and fresh environments. These people may get bored when they think that things always remain the unchanged and nothing fresh seems to happen.

As a good leader, you should learn try to identify how each of your team members react to change. Your change management plan should include steps that could help members to deal with the change at hand. If you fail to consider how your people may respond to change, you may face any or all of these problems: intense dissatisfaction, anxiety, skepticism, doubt, defiance against the change (for stability-oriented persons) and defiance against the status quo (for change-oriented persons), and irrationality of actions.

- **Every member of the team has essential needs that need to be addressed.**

Dr. Will Schultz, a renowned psychologist, has ascertained that people normally have three fundamental needs when it comes to interpersonal relationships. These fundamental needs are greatly important when people are forced to face a change: the need to control, the need to be included and the need for honesty.

The intensity of these needs actually varies from one person to the other. But regardless of the intensity, these needs have to be addressed during change management.

- People need to feel that they are in control of their own future.

- People need to feel that they are somehow involved in the development of the change that is about to take place.

- People need to feel that their superiors are being honest and open about the details of the change.

If your change management plan fails to include any of these innate needs, you may be faced with an assortment of negative response from your members. These negative responses can be as mild as indifference but can be as serious as absolute hostility.

- **Almost all changes entail a certain kind of loss.**

Some form of loss is almost always inevitable when there is change. These losses resulting from change also greatly vary. For someone who is promoted to a higher post, the form of loss that that person experience is the loss of his or her old position that had become secure and comfortable. Yes, this kind of loss is a good kind of loss because the person has a new and better job to compensate for the lost job. But the loss can be greater or more serious in other change situations. One example is when a company needs to reduce its manpower by letting go of some of its trusted employees. The devastating losses from this change can include lost income, lost relationships and even lost self-esteem.

People who suffer from losses normally undergo a pattern called the "loss curve" – shock, anger, rejection, acceptance and then finally healing.

As a good leader, you need to understand how you can help your people to go through the loss curve. You need to prepare yourself and your team for the shock or the denial stage that the new change may bring. More importantly, you also need to know how you can help your members to deal with the possible feelings of anger and reject that they have due to the new change. You need to have a plan that includes enough time for your company and your people to adjust to the new situation.

- **Expectations should be handled reasonably.**

You must have experienced the frustration and disappointment yourself when the thing you expect did not materialize. This same principle applies to your team members during times of change. If you gave them false expectations, whether intentionally or unintentionally, you can certainly expect some form of frustration and disappointment from them. But if you stick with the facts and have always communicated the truth to your team, you will be able to level their expectations and at the same time help them to find the best option available for them.

If, for example, you need to shutdown one part of your operations, you need to be honest enough with your team if you think there will be redundancies that will be put into effect. Don't sugarcoat your message which can make them expect job security when there is actually none. It is better to tell them outright that they might lose their jobs so they can do the necessary actions to find a new one. As a good leader, avoid making promises that you know you cannot keep. It is always better to face the truth and handle the situation immediately. Your problems will just become bigger when you delay telling the truth to your people.

- **Fears are expected and should be properly handled.**

When your organization has to face an important change, logical thinking is normally one of the first things that disappear. When they hear that a significant change is about to happen, many people start to think of the worst things that could happen. They suddenly fear a lot of things - losing their jobs, not finding a new job soon enough, losing their homes when they aren't able to pay their mortgages, losing their loved ones when they cannot give them a good life, losing face for the disgrace they will give their children. These fears can mutate into bigger fears when left unchecked.

As a good leader, you should make sure that these fears are immediately addressed. You need to provide encouragement to your people and tell them that despite the impending losses, they will always be able to find a solution to their problems.

Here are a few tips you can use when applying the key principles of change management:

- Always give your team members enough information. Don't let your team members to guess, it can turn out into uncontrollable gossips and speculations. Instead, be open and truthful about the details of the imminent change. But beware of giving very optimistic promises that can lead to disappointments. It is better to stick with the facts so that your team members will not expect anything more than you can provide.

- If you have a big organization, take time in creating a communication strategy that will allow you to communicate all information with efficiency. Without an efficient strategy, the rumor mill that exists in your organization will surely take over. As much as possible, communicate details to everyone simultaneously. Then you can setup follow-up sessions with smaller groups so you can personally communicate your plans and strategies. Through this small group sessions, you will be able to identify any reactions from various individuals and determine the appropriate way to deal with these reactions.

- As much as possible, give your members a chance to choose for themselves. But you need to clearly and honestly inform them about the possible outcomes of their choices.

- Allot enough time for your people to process the information and to convey their point of view. Give your members the opportunity to express any issues or concerns that they may have about the change. Make sure that you are ready to give reassurances for the issues and concerns raised by your team. This encouragement can definitely make them feel more comfortable about the impending change.

- If there are choices to be made, you need to make sure that there is enough support system that can help your people make the right choice. If you need to hire outside help who can provide coaching and counseling to your own people, consider doing so.

- If the change you are about to make entails some loss, determine what alternative you can provide as replacement for the loss. Your people will find it easier to deal with the possibility of loss if they know that will gain something in return. Have a replacement can help lessen any possible fears that your members might feel about the change.

If the change you plan to embark on is big in nature, such as relocating to another location or implementing a new system, you should handle the change as a project. The success of the change will greatly rely on how effectively you can implement the project management process that involves setting up a project management team, creating plans and timelines, distributing resources.

Chapter 8: Becoming the Leader You Want To Be

"Before you are a leader, success is all about growing yourself. When you become a leader, success is all about growing others"

- Jack Welch

With great power comes great responsibility, how many times have we heard this adage but have refused to acknowledge its significance holistically. Leadership is a quality that only few have by birth. It needs to be worked upon and built on, piece by piece. It is not merely a title, it a way of being, a way of living. To live up to the role of a leader, you must believe that you can be the leader that you want to be.

Being a leader VS becoming a leader

"Leadership is unlocking people's potential to become better."

- Bill Bradley

There is a sea of differences between being a leader and becoming a leader. In order for you to maximize your potential and be the leader you have always wanted to be you need to realize and accept which category you belong to.

While some leaders are born, some work to lead. And it is in this essential difference in how leadership is acquired that the fate of success or failure is decided. Different environment and different atmospheres require a different kind of approach towards leadership.

In the work space, you might not voluntarily choose to lead but the responsibility might fall on you. In such a situation, you must learn how to become a leader. The first part of this process is recognizing your assets and your weaknesses. After that, diagram you surroundings and find your weakest and strongest points, as a team. Then, study the work that you have been assigned and delegate work. And finally ensure that all goes smoothly and according to plan.

Map your own self

The most important part of being the leader you want to be, is to be completely in tune with your own fault lines. There is no need to hide your imperfections as they make you human and recognizing as well as accepting them, enhances your perception as a leader. A leader does not lead the crème de la crème, his job is to bring together the best in everyone so as to fulfill targets and achieve success. This is why staying ignorant of your own problems will only make it harder for you to lead other. Your weaknesses can make you vulnerable if you don't address them at the right time.

At the same time, make most of your best qualities. Do not shy from accepting what you can do best even if you think it is trivial. This will help you in concentrating on doing that which you like and are good at while at the same time, giving you the space to supervise everyone else. But you must be careful not to be boastful as a pompous leader is the worst kind. You will not only put off your team, you will also channel negativity and jealousy into your colleagues.

Sync with your atmosphere

Your most important task as a leader is to be completely in sync with your atmosphere. This does not only mean the material surroundings but also comprehending fully the composition of your team. This will allow you to extract maximum potential from the people you are working with. Do not focus too much on what you lack as a team, rather shift focus to what all you can easily achieve. Be completely honest with the people who make up your team.

For instance, in the first meeting itself, talk about what part of the project each person would like to work on. While you discuss this, note the contradictions and similarities in each personality. If you can or want to work in groups, use this knowledge to make up those groups and give to each the task that they would be most comfortable with.

However, as a leader, it is your responsibility to push people out of their comfort zone too. If you feel that a certain member of your team has the potential but is hesitant to take up the work, encourage him to try and accept it as a challenge. In case the person succeeds, then that's great for not only your team but is also an immense boost to the self confidence of that person but in case he doesn't, then do not make a big deal about it and just have an honest conversation about where he lacked and what more he could've done. If you see the possibility as viable, you could even give the member a second chance.

Know your goal

In spite of the overwhelming work you might have to do to become the leader, you still have one very important task left. A leader is supposed to lead his team to success, which is to the successful achievement of a certain goal. But in the hustle bustle of all the work that goes around the post of a leader, it is easy to forget why you were made the leader in the first place.

Effective leadership must include a very clear idea of how work must be distributed and delegated. As mentioned in the previous point, it would be ideal to begin with assigning everyone with what they are most comfortable with as long as it ensures the successful completion of the whole project. You might have to push people to try new things and work with greater efficiency but that is your cross to bear and bear it you must.

A good leader does not hold back on either praise or criticism, so be free with both. If you feel things are not being done the way you want them to, voice your concern in the clearest way possible. Holding back now might cost you the whole project eventually.

Supervision

For most, this is all that there is to being a leader, but unfortunately, it is only a very small part of a rather important and tasking job. Ensuring everyone does their work might cost you a lot of emotional and mental stress, but it needs to be done. Your leadership resides in the following of your team and if they cannot accept and respect your authority, then it compromises your role as an effective leader.

Chapter 9: Strategies to Become an Incredible Leader

"If your actions inspire others to dream more, learn more, do more and become more, you are a leader."

- John Quincy Adams

Incredible leadership doesn't happen in a day's time. It takes immense efforts and a level of consistency to get there. Leadership can be extremely detrimental to the success or failure of a business.

Incredible leaders won't let you know how much they may have struggled to get wherever they are right now. They just make it seem so easy. Great leadership doesn't come easy to anybody and no one is born with all those qualities.

The below mentioned aspects will give you an insight of what goes into being a great leader.

Take Control

Regardless of the circumstances around you, as a great leader you need to take charge of such situations. Ensure that you take responsibility for your own failures and success at work. You need to stop getting complacent and ask yourself what is that you are doing to change things around you. Only you can develop your potential by finding out ways to reach your goals.

Identify your strengths

It's essential to know the strengths and weaknesses of your personality. Knowing your flaws could help you identify where you are lacking and gives you a great opportunity to work on them. Similarly, when you are aware of your strengths, you can utilize them to meet your goals at work. For instance, you may be good at people management. This particular plus point of your personality will help you convince your clients about your ideas. You can sit down and make a note of all these pros and cons of your personality. Accordingly you can figure out how to work on fixing or enhancing them.

Be a Visionary

If you aspire to be the best, you need to be a visionary. As a leader, you need to create a vision for your organization and encourage people to work towards it. This vision needs to be precise and clear; without that it is impossible to achieve success. A vision statement is basically a picture of where you would want to be in the future. This will constantly remind you of your goals and motivate you to work on it. It's easier when you break your vision into smaller goals and chalk out a plan to accomplish it.

Motivate Others

Leaders not only focus on their own personal growth but also motivate others to create that same level of passion amongst your subordinates. Their positivity makes their colleagues seek advice from them on important matters. People trust their leaders in helping them make the right choice. They strongly believe that their leader possesses extraordinary qualities that can be very useful for them and they seek strength and motivation from the leader.

Become more visible

For your efforts to gain acceptance, you need to be more visible among your peers. It is also a great way to build a rapport with them and know if they are unhappy with a particular aspect of the organization's management. Also participate in company events to let other know who you really are and what difference you can make to their success. Your inhibitions will only lead to misunderstandings and you won't be taken seriously by others. You need to ooze that confidence that will make others take notice of you.

Bond with your seniors

Forming a strong relationship with your seniors will enhance your knowledge and help you look at things from a different perspective. Utilize their expertise and do not hesitate to consult them in case you are caught up in difficult situations. Do not be intimidated by their positions and try building a healthy relationship with them. Remember, you are not doing this to use their influence but only to gain their acquired knowledge through various experiences. It is of utmost importance that you identify them as equals and have them as a much needed support for enhancing your career.

Channelize your energies in a positive way

This could be a great motivating factor that can easily help you meet your goals. For instance, you may have suffered some traumatic incidents in life which you may feel extremely angry about. The moment you are reminded of that incident, you may begin to clench your fist or feel a slight fire in your tummy. You need to channelize this anger in you and push yourself to do more good work. When you break away from your restraints, you will come out feeling more powerful, positive and confident about yourself than ever. This anger of yours can keep that passion burning inside you to be a successful person.

Get rid of your fears

We all know that fears are transient. However we still experience it in almost every walk of life. In case of leaders, it could hinder them from implementing new ideas that could take them to greater heights. The most common fear when you are a leader is the fear of voicing your opinions assuming it may lead to something worse and you could get ridiculed for the same. When you fear something, just ask yourself whether your fears are realistic enough for you to put in so much time worrying about them? And if at all they are true, what's the worst that can happen? You would rather want to take actions and give your aspirations a try instead of mulling over things you could have done to make your life better.

Keep looking for new possibilities

If you notice that a certain colleague is doing a job that you would like to take up, let your superiors know. Do something about it when you feel like you are stuck in a rut. Identify your strengths and always look out for new opportunities that can showcase your skills. For instance, if you like training people, volunteer to conduct refresher sessions for your colleagues on a particular topic. You can also ask the seniors if you can carry out a special presentation on topics that would benefit the whole organization.

Be Positive

You are ought to have ups and downs in your career. You may feel disheartened as not everything can work out as per your plans. It's alright to feel that way, but it's essential to quickly get back on track by accepting these failures. It's only human to easily get discouraged but only an incredible leader knows how to turn around such situation to your favor.

When you realize your true potential and are willing to take it to a level par excellence, you can truly be an incredible leader.

Chapter 10: Qualities Team Members Look for in a Leader

"A leader is best when people barely know he exists, when his work is done, his aim fulfilled, they will say, we did it ourselves"

- Lao Tzu

Good leaders need to be of a strong and decent character. You would want people to look up to you for all the exceptional qualities you possess and follow your lead. People are always looking for a good role model who they can emulate and find peace in knowing that they have somebody to guide them. Everyone wants to feel assured that their growth and future is in good hands.

Let's look at the qualities people, especially team members look for in their leader.

Proper Communication

People need somebody who can clearly define the work expected out of them. As a leader you need to lay down precise strategies and discuss them with the subordinates. You need to be open to suggestions and give timely and constructive feedback to them. People are not fond of leaders who are aloof and somebody who only preaches to them. They need a guide who can support them through all their endeavors by constantly being communicative with them.

Connect with people

You may possess all the great leadership qualities that make a good leader, but you would not be able to accomplish anything without having a connection with the people. People need to identify with you more and feel that you care about them. Instead of sending congratulatory mails to your subordinates, it's always advisable to walk up to them and give a pat on their back.

They need to feel that their efforts are being appreciated and given their due importance. You could start with saying a simple hello to your staff when you walk in, or ask them how they spend their weekend. Slowly you will notice that your employees will be more than willing to share their ideas and show more interest in their work. If your employees feel they can approach you in case of any issues, you will have happier people in your office. These happy attitudes will in turn lead to greater work efficiency.

Provide with tools for developing their skills

Ensure that you provide your staff with the best trainings wherever needed and technology as much as possible. This will make their work easier and they won't feel exhausted. Provide them with all the relevant training that can give them extra knowledge or opportunities for growth. You can also tie-up with certain educational institutions and fund their course fees. These things will gain a sense of achievement in them and they will feel valued. Very rarely will your employees think about joining a different organization, if they feel they have a higher chance of growth in your company.

Ready to learn

A good leader is always ready to learn new things and adapt them in their ways of working. A leader can never get too complacent and needs to be updated with the latest technologies. It can be through various blogs, journals, forums or websites that could help the business grow. As a leader, you always want your team to mirror you. When they notice your desire for learning they may soon start following you. As a result you will have smarter employees who would have all the knowledge to overcome their difficulties.

Listen to employees

People do not want leaders who go on preaching about things. They need someone who can also listen to what they have to say. Being a good listener will also keep you well-informed about the needs of your employees. You may even be surprised to know that they might have some excellent ideas or strategies that could help grow your business. If ever you come across one of your best employees lacking in performance, you can simply have a one-on-one chat with him and find out if something else is bothering him. This could also prove to be helpful in building a stronger connect with them.

Proper Implementation of Change

Any change in the system needs to be carefully and wisely implemented without causing a chaos. A leader must ensure that there is a smooth transmission from one level to another while embracing the change. Similarly it's important to precisely convey your employees about the same. The leader needs to come up with the most creative ways to make it easier for everyone in the organization to adapt to the change in the system. There is also a need for explaining them the benefits and need for the new strategies that will be implemented. That way, people will look forward to it as a tool to enhance their skills rather than being reluctant about it.

Accept Responsibilities

A diligent leader will always accept additional responsibilities that no one would take up. You need to set an example for your employees to be ready to put in that extra effort at crucial times. Treat your work like you would want other to treat theirs. This will make them look up to you and follow your path.

Accept failures

We all make mistakes, but very few of us actually accept them and own up to their faults. It is always humbling to see your leader own up to his mistakes and display such level of transparency. Admitting your failures is the first step towards ensuring that you won't repeat them in the future and improving the situation. Failures can teach you how to cope in the most difficult situations only to come out as a winner. On the other hand by not accepting your drawbacks and passing the blame will only result in more mudslinging without really focusing at the problem on hand. You will not be paying attention towards rectifying the mistakes but rather waste time playing blame games.

Integrity

One cannot under-estimate the importance of being honest towards their organization. Integrity can go a long way in defining your success both personally and professionally. Truthfulness is not just an endearing quality but needs you to be honest at all time regardless of your situation. Manipulation in all forms needs to be avoided to be able to have a clear conscience and true inner and external growth of a leader.

Humility

Being humble to others at all times reflects how secure you are without the need to feel intimidated by others. If you go wrong at times, admit that you indeed failed and you may not have all the right answers. Adopting this attitude indicates that it is never too late to start learning.

Courage

A great leader is always ready to take on risks to accomplish the goals of the organization. He or she is equipped with a high sense of judgment that rarely fails. The leader is well aware of the things he would be risking if he takes that plunge. Hence it's less likely that his decisions would go wrong.

Unbiased

You need to treat people with equal respect regardless of their position or expertise. Be sensitive towards everybody and do not ignore anyone. There should be no difference in your body language while you are speaking to the security guard of the company or a CEO. Each person deserves to be respected for whatever they have achieved in their lives and career.

As a leader, you need to keep in mind the qualities that people seek from their leader because living up to the expectation of the team and the management along with achieving organizational goals will make you a competent and an efficient leader. Do not underestimate the requirements of your team from you as a leader because your success as a leader lies in the success they achieve when performing the tasks that are assigned to them.

Chapter 11: Incredible Leaders from History

Social psychology and Sociology describe leadership as a process or theory through which a person, known as leader influences, guides and motivates his or her team members to get involved in a particular task and to work on the path of achieving the goal/mission of the team. Thus a leader is person with leadership qualities. These qualities are varied and include charisma, decisiveness, intelligence, smartness etc; all of these make a normal person a good leader.

Sometimes even environmental factors, i.e. circumstances and such are quite important in making of a successful leader. Thus the above definition is quite important as it is universally acknowledged and accepted, but if studied thoroughly one may see that the definition falls short at some places. The definition fails to denote the paths and ways of leaders who are considered to be the greatest among the greatest.

As explained above, a great leader has some essential qualities. Yet not every great leader becomes a legendary leader, the leader among the leaders. What makes some of the leaders the best among the best? The answer is their uniqueness; every leader has something unique about them which if developed properly can make them one of the best leaders. These leaders guide masses to innovation and new ideas and thus revolutions happen.

Since the ancient times, we have been blessed with legendary leaders. These leaders led their people effectively and made their masses loved as well as respect them. These leaders turned out to be so great that even today they are respected or remembered all over the world.

These efficient men as well as women ushered their masses into new worlds, new beginnings and new lives. Right from the ancient Egyptian Civilization to today's modern world there have been many great leaders, such as Buddha, Hatshepsut, Alexander, Asoka, Louis XIV, Akbar, Gandhi, Martin Luther King, etc and even now, when the times have changed the contributions of these ancient as well as modern and postmodern leaders still are remembered and their leadership theories can be used to make more and more legendary leaders. Let us look at some of the most influential and path breaking leaders who with their leadership qualities changed the theory of being a leader.

Prophet Muhammad

One of the greatest medieval leaders, Prophet Muhammad not only spread one of the most widespread religions of all times but also united his people against various things. He not only spread Islam in Arabia but directly or indirectly helped Islam to spread all over the world. His contributions to spreading of Islam can be seen today as Islam is the second largest and also the fastest growing religion of the world. He united his people who were in a chaotic state and made them understand humanity, peace and morality. He helped his people out of persecution and other problems. He led some of the largest migrations in the human history and made them successful. He led many successful wars and defeated and conquered larger armies just with his legendary leadership qualities. These qualities are courage, bravery, leading by example, persistence and decisiveness.

Julius Caesar

You can understand the importance of this man by the fact that he gave his name to the month of July. Caesar was a deadly combo; he was not only one of the greatest military leaders but also one of the best political leaders in the history of mankind. He led several victorious campaigns and fought many battles and increased the boundaries of the Roman Empire single handedly making it one of the most prosperous dynasties ever. He revolutionized the Roman government and laid the foundation of the great Roman Empire. He did all of this with the help of his bold and brave attitude, his eager and opportunists behavior and good sense of strategic planning.

Mahatma Gandhi

The frail, old man who led thousands of Indians on the path of freedom from the British Empire was originally named Mohandas Karamchand Gandhi, but due to his immense works and leadership qualities he came to be known as Mahatma, the great soul. An ordinary boy with a dream of being extraordinary, Gandhi worked hard and led the Indian freedom struggle. He with his weapons of non violence or ahimsa forced the British Imperialists to back off and made India an independent nation. His silent approach, etc led India to freedom finally in the year 1947.

Mao Zedong

The founder of Maoism, Mao was the leader of the Chinese Revolutions who is also considered to be the founding father of the People's Republic of China. He successfully repelled the Japanese invasion in the World War 2 and led China on the path of industrial and economical revolution. He is one of the major reasons because of which China is considered to be one of the super nations of not only Asia but across the world.

Nelson Mandela

The first South African President who got elected in a fully democratic election, the late Nelson Mandela is one of the strongest modern leaders. Mandela also had a lion's share in the anti apartheid movements in South Africa and also served a really lengthy term in prison for his beliefs. He devoted his life for uniting his country and did it after serving 30 years in prison. His determination, perseverance and courage are praiseworthy.

Winston Churchill

One of the strongest Prime Ministers to grace the Great Britain, Winston Churchill stayed in his post for five years; from 1940 to 1945 .Churchill led the Great Britain against the Nazi Germany strongly during the World War 2. He collaborated with the allies and was one of the main reasons which led to the downfall of Hitler. He became the prime minster of Great Britain in a time when the world was in great chaos and people were afraid of the destruction caused by Fuhrer and his pals. Winston Churchill was famous for his bold and fearless attitude, his can-do personality and his determination knew no bounds.

George Washington

One of the four founding fathers of the United States of America, George Washington was the leader of the American Revolution and also technically the first president of the United States of America. His foresight, vision and planning are some of the qualities which should be studied to understand his leadership. His ability to lead and influence people is also one of his major leadership qualities.

Abraham Lincoln

The most famous and well known leader of all time, Abraham Lincoln was the 16th president of the United States of America. He is also rightly considered to be the most brilliant president of America. His struggles and toils and his story of becoming the president of one of the most powerful nations is repeated all over the world and motivates everyone. He came in position when the United States of America was undergoing the American Civil War, but he with his amiable leadership qualities prevented America breaking into shards. He ended slavery by signing the Emancipation Proclamation and thus made himself loved all over. Though he was assassinated, his leadership qualities still are motivating people. His major qualities were determination, perseverance, self control and strong sense of nationality.

Fidel Castro

Another controversial yet strong leader, Fidel Castro led the Cuban Revolution. He then became the prime minister of Cuba and stayed in the position from 1976 to 2008. Enduring many crisis, assassination attempts, invasions etc, Castro led his people strongly. He has proven to be a strong and a motivated leader. His courage, strategy, correct decisions etc made him one of the most famous personalities of the modern world.

All of these leaders led their people strongly on the path of success. They with their amiable and glorious leadership qualities became some of the greatest personalities of the world. They conquered their difficulties, defeated their foes and influenced their pals. Their leadership qualities and theories are well studied and followed all over the world, thus making them some of the most glorious people in the history of mankind.

Chapter 12: Leave Your Legacy

"Everyone must leave something behind when he dies . . . Something your hand touched some way so your soul has somewhere to go when you die . . . It doesn't matter what you do, so long as you change something from the way it was before you touched it into something that's like you after you take your hands away."
- Ray Bradbury, Fahrenheit 451

One sad truth is that there are a lot of good and effective leaders in the corporate world who ended their leadership career with nothing to show for it. Yes, people may remember their names but other than that, they usually end up forgotten. On the other hand, there are other leaders who were not necessarily exceptional or effective who were able to leave behind a legacy. Even after several generations, their names and the changes that they have made are often repeated.

What is the secret of these leaders that allowed them not only to create an influence during their journey but to carry on in changing the lives of many people and organizations even long after they have gone? What did they do that the flames they started were kept alive generation after generation?

Some people will readily say that the secret is basic exposure. When you are the CEO or the leader of a company that belongs to the Fortune 100, it definitely gives you a leverage to have your leadership standards circulated to a wider range of audience. Of course, you will have a harder time to do this if you are leading a small company that only has one or two branches or locations.

Yes, exposure certainly has its advantages. But there are a lot of CEOs from Fortune 100 companies who have not left a legacy. The hard truth is that some leaders are really just better in providing leadership and in creating and inspiring a legacy.

If you want to be remembered long after you have left the organization you are leading, there are ways how you can do it. If you sincerely want to make a long-lasting transformation in the organization or the industry you are currently working in, here are the techniques on how you can do it:

- **Recognize what truly matters.**
You cannot really expect to leave behind a legacy by mistake or by accident. If you are truly sincere about your intentions, you will not stop searching until you unmistakably and definitely know that one thing that you want to change and leave behind. You need to determine what kind of legacy you want to leave behind. You will not be able to move forward to the next steps of building your legacy unless you clearly know what it is.

It doesn't really matter what field or area you want to focus on. You may want to create a new culture in your organization, or to dramatically improve the quality of your products, or to transform how you provide customer service. There are a lot of options you can choose from. But the most important thing is for you to know what that one thing that you want to accomplish is.

Once you have determined the kind of legacy you want to leave behind, it is advisable to write all your ideas on paper. Write a policy, a program or a proposal for it. Have it printed and distributed to your key employees. Discuss it with them and get their inputs. Continuously revise your plan until you feel sure that that is what you want to do. Take away anything that doesn't sound right or doesn't really fit. The objective is to have a clear and definite plan.

- **Leave the front line.**

Now that you have a clear and definite plan, you need to let go and let things happen. Talk with your team, with your managers and supervisors and clearly lay down the plan with them. After that, you will need to give them space to carry out the details of your plan. Don't involve yourself with the tedious details of implementing your plan. That is the role of your managers and supervisors. In order for you to leave a legacy, you always have to look at the big picture and see how things are turning out from a higher perspective.

If you need to, find a Chief Operating Officer (COO) who can handle the operations for you. Learn how to delegate. However when you decide to implement your plans of leaving a legacy, you need to understand that you need to leave the front line. What you need to focus on and spend most of your time with are the people who work for you, especially your managers and supervisors.

Empower your people. Teach them how to do things the right way. Inspire them to become better people. Help them learn how to capitalize on their strengths and improve on their weaknesses. This is the most important part of your legacy building. This is how people will remember you.

- **Keep repeating your vision up to the point of making everyone sick.**

Yes, you understood it correctly. If you look at how the greatest leaders were able to build a long-lasting legacy, you will see that they all did the same thing. They continuously repeated their vision and plans to their teams. They do it every day. They sometimes do it more than once every day. They do so vocally and through their actions. They repeat the vision and plans during meetings. They again repeat them when talking to their people on a one on one basis. They reiterate it during performance assessments. They remind everyone again during general assemblies. Those leaders were persistent and unrelenting in inculcating their vision and plans to their team.

You need to understand that great leaders do this for several years, sometimes even for a couple of decades. Nothing worth achieving can be done overnight. You have to commit to doing this for as long as required. And you have to do it ceaselessly and without a break. Only through this way can you truly build a lasting legacy.

- **Leave while you are ahead.**

One obvious fact that many good leaders miss is that leaving a legacy means that you actually have to leave for it to be called a legacy. Unfortunately many leaders miss this one important point. After reaching their peak, they choose to stay longer in the limelight. They lingered too long that the impact of their legacy has greatly diminished why they were still present. Do yourself a favor by relinquishing your throne while you are at the top of your game. You can always find something else to focus your attention to.

Chapter 13: Lead By Example!

Too often have I experienced those who believe the root of "leading" lies within the crack of their whip.

That is to say, they believe leading is done by telling others what to do, accomplished usually by means of intimidation or fear. This is not a solid way to lead for numerous reasons:

1. People can only take so much

For most, being yelled at or intimidated constantly wears them down physically and emotionally. Eventually their bodies or their minds will falter leaving either diminished results or a complete stoppage all-together. It's definitely not going to enhance them in any way, shape, or form. But rather tear them down and keep them from any means of improvement.

2. The strong-minded may revolt

The true "sheep" of the herd will surely wither away into nothing, until they can no longer. But it's the silent leaders that you need worry about. Eventually rumblings will arise through your followers, and they will grow angry and bitter. So much so that they may confront you about it, sometimes physically. Most often however, they will do something to show they won't stand for this behavior any longer.

In a work environment this may mean working to rule, striking, or even quitting their jobs.

3. Do as I say, not as I do

Don't talk the talk, if you aren't willing to walk the walk. People will see this and you will lose all your credibility in a heartbeat. Your words will fall on deaf ears as people no longer value what you have to say. It's very important to practice what you preach in order to instill those beliefs firmly in the minds of those whom you are looking to change or convince.

For example, don't say "Cussing will NOT be tolerated in this environment" yet you cuss wildly whenever you are angered or upset. It shows people how they are supposed to act when they are angry or upset, and ultimately influences their behavior.

I have personally been forced under many "dictators" who choose to talk over perform, so I have definitely seen both sides to this equation. The major issue that they all had in common was a lack of performance, even if it meant unsuccessful business ventures, losing profit, or just straight losing. All of the teams had so much more potential that went virtually untapped due to the horrendous leadership offered. In some cases people were not only kept from reaching their full potential, but they were actually hindered and got worse over time rather than better.

What you must do instead is to <u>lead by example.</u>

Yes is sounds so cliché and yet it is the most vital aspect of good leadership. Most people learn visually and by doing whatever it is that needs to be done. So by actually performing said task, you are setting a proper example of what they should be doing as well.

Also you can set the benchmark standards for production. It's easy to say "Work harder!" or "You are not working hard enough!". While quite frankly people don't buy that for a second. If you simply say that they could and should be working harder, without actually doing the work yourself, then people will think you have unrealistic expectations and don't know what you are talking about, since you have not experienced what they are doing first hand. Yet if you actually do the work and show by example the amount of effort that should be given, then people will have no choice but to match your speed and proficiency. Often even pushing to out-do you!

Here's 10 ways one can lead by example:

- Take Responsibility – Even when it's not your fault. When you show others that you are willing to take the blame for their mistakes, it gives them a whole new grasp on who you are. And most undoubtedly will cause them to work head over heels to repay your kindness.

- Be truthful – Sounds simple but can often be very difficult. The key here is to be truthful, without being ruthless. Give praise whenever it's due, and deal with problems gently but honestly.

- Be courageous - *"Strength and Honor" - Gladiator*

- Acknowledge Failure – It allows your team to understand that failure is a part of life, but it is how we push through it and keep working to succeed that defines us.

- Be Persistent - *"Don't give up, don't ever give up"* *- Jim Valvano*. Still chokes me up when I hear it.

If you are unaware Jim Valvano was a legendary leader of men, and coached NC State to a National Championship in 1983. They beat the terrifying University of Houston who were lead by future hall of famers Clyde Drexler and Hakeem Olajuwon in one of the greatest upsets in college basketball history.

He said this during a speech he gave at the ESPY's in March of 1993. His body, ravaged by cancer and barely unable to walk, stood there in defiance of his condition and delivered one of the greatest speeches of all time.

He died 8 weeks later, but has raised over 100 million dollars to date through his charity, The V Foundation, for cancer research.

- Create Solutions – Don't dwell on problems, but rather be creative and excited about discovering solutions.

- Listen – Be quick to listen, and slow to speak. Ask questions and truly listen to what others have to say. Not only will you gain much respect by valuing what others have to say, but you'll also learn a great deal in the process.

- Delegate Liberally – Encourage an atmosphere in which people can focus on their core strengths.

- Take Care of yourself - Exercise, don't overwork, and remember to take a break. A balanced team, mentally and physically, is a successful team. Model it, encourage it, support it!

- Roll Up your Sleeve – Like leading your men into battle, you'll inspire greatness in your company!

Conclusion

Thank you once again for downloading this eBook and reading through. I hope that after reading this eBook, you are now ready to take on to your role as a leader in a much more effective and efficient manner.

Your inherent skills as a leader and the tips from this eBook will bring about a major change in your leadership skills. These will not just enhance your skills as a leader but will also improve your interpersonal relationships with your team members. You will be able to motivate and inspire them to achieve their organizational goals in a better manner.

Congratulations for having all the tools that are needed to become an efficient and an effective leader that people can't help but follow. You will lead them from front and drive from within the team.

The next step for you is to take to heart all that you have read and understood and start implementing the same at the workplace. You will be astonished with the amazing changes you will see in yourself as a leader; starting now, you are not just a leader, you are a leader who can make a difference.

Made in the USA
San Bernardino, CA
29 September 2015